THE SWEETEST ROSE OF TEXAS

The Life Poetry and Teachings of
Lois Pauline Moore-Newcomb

Lois Pauline Moore-Newcomb

WestBow
PRESS
A DIVISION OF THOMAS NELSON

cover image by Monika Moore
art.monikamoore@yahoo.com

WestBow Press books may be ordered through booksellers or by contacting:

WestBow Press
A Division of Thomas Nelson
1663 Liberty Drive
Bloomington, IN 47403
www.westbowpress.com
1-(866) 928-1240

Scripture taken from the King James Version of the Bible.

ISBN: 978-1-4497-9750-8 (sc)
ISBN: 978-1-4497-9749-2 (e)

Library of Congress Control Number: 2013910264

Printed in the United States of America.

WestBow Press rev. date: 6/10/2013

FORWARD BY
MESSIANIC RABBI JAY NEWCOMB

I wish peace and long life to all who read this book. After Mother's late teen years, she did not record anymore of her personal experiences. She had a hard life and perhaps it was more than she could bear to recall. I know that she had a miscarriage and lost a child early in her first marriage. Orbie Hiser suffered through years of epileptic seizures and finally passed away leaving her alone with my brothers and sisters; David, Paul, Linda and Glenda.

But she met my Father, Edward M. Newcomb, from Baltimore, Maryland in Church and sometime later they were married. I was born in 1964 in Deming, New Mexico. They traveled much and spent a good deal of time moving from place to place. They moved between Gulfport, Mississippi and Joplin, Missouri. Also they moved between Wickenburg, Arizona and Deming New Mexico. San Antonio and Pharr, Texas, then on up to El Paso; finally here to Carlsbad where my Father, who was ill with COPD and a stomach rupture, passed away in August of 1973. I am not sure of the time sequence of all these moves except they last two were in 1969 and 1970. The reasons for these moves were, for the most part, the fact that my Father was a Baptist Preacher. It may seem funny that a Messianic Rabbi has a Baptist Preacher for a Father, but I followed a different path and this story is not about me but her.

Her oldest son David, my brother passed away of Cancer in Portland, Oregon in July of 2011, and she greaves for her son. She lives now at Landsun Nursing home in Carlsbad, New Mexico. On April 12th, 2013, she was 92 years old.

To you dear and beloved Mother, from all of your children, we love you very much. And from all of the Grand children and Great Grandchildren, they all love you and in you they are well blessed.

I have placed these poems in the book by chronological sequence and some reflect the emotions and feelings that she had at the time; the exception being the one where she records how God spoke to her and how He placed His calling upon her life. The ones which were undated, I have placed at the beginning of her book. She is also a song writer and two of her songs were published by columbine records. "Just Because," and, "Use Us Now Dear Lord In Thy Service For Thee." She has a deep abiding faith in G-d and tried her best to instill that in all of us as we were growing up. She attended Bethel Baptist Church for years, and when she could no longer drive and walk, she was unable to attend anymore. It is to the shame of these people that once she was unable to attend services, they all but forgot about her. But she loves them all the same and there is no malice in her heart.

So here are the written words of faith of Mrs. Lois Pauline-Moore Newcomb, beloved Queen of our family. Shalom.

Rabbi Jay P. Newcomb 1 March 2013.

MY LIFE AND STORY

I'm Lois. I was born on April 21st, 1921, in Dallas County Texas. Now here in 2012 I am ninety-two years old living here in Carlsbad, New Mexico. I Have for quite a number of years. I moved here in 1970 with my second husband, Reverend Edward M. Newcomb, and our little son Jay. My daughter Glenda was still at home then also. She was the youngest of the four from my first husband, David Orbie Hiser. He passed away from a massive heart attack on Oct 7, 1957. He had a damaged heart do to epilepsy. He had taken that illness after a fall from the roof of the store we ran in Mesquite. Our children were David, Paul, Linda and Glenda.

It wasn't too long after we came to Carlsbad with my 2nd husband to Pastor Faith Chapel Freewill Baptist Church that Linda came home from Dallas. She met us here in Carlsbad, where she married my son-in-law, Kenneth Tanner. My husband Eddy passed away here on August 22nd 1973, and I've lived here ever since. Jay was nine when Eddy passed away, and I raised him until he left to join the army. But he's home now after twenty-eight years away, and I'm living here in the nursing home.

I recall much from my life. I want to share those memories with all my kids, grandchildren and great grandchildren, so they'll know what it was like for us in those days.

When I was three I was taken to the hospital for surgery to remove my tonsils. My father held me before going into surgery. That was in 1924. I was scared to death, but I came through it ok and my father and mother were always there for me.

As a small child I was afraid of the dark. There were no streetlights out on the farm and we lit our home with oil lamps. We didn't have electricity then. My parents told me I used to sleep walk and would go outside. Father and Mother would follow me around outside making sure I didn't get hurt. Then they would follow along as I walked back to my bed

A man in a mule-drawn wagon used to come to the farm where we lived. He was a peddler selling sewing machines. He picked up rugs as well and left over sewing materials. He would come by and holler, "Ah rag man, ah rag man! Rag mops rag mops!" I remember when I would misbehave mother would say, "Straighten up or rag man will get you."

When my brother Odell and I were small, he was two and I was 6, we lived in this big two-story house. It had a big metal attic that Odell and I would climb up to on the ladder. But we were afraid to go farther than the top of the ladder so we wouldn't go into the attic.

We also liked to sing. Odell would sing the high notes and I the harmonizing ones. I still like to sing. There at the farm was a big huge tree that stood out in front of the house between it and the road. There was a rope swing with a Cassin tied on the end. That was what a car tire was called back in those days. We would swing in it real high and sing, "Swing low, swing high, sweet chariot, coming forth to carry me home."

When I was seven years old, I started school in Mesquite wearing my first store bought dress. I thought that was the prettiest dress I had ever seen. It came a little above my knees.

When I was ten, my parents bought me a pretty red lace up shoes. They came up to just a little bit above my ankles. They were a bright red color and I was so proud of those shoes.

Our home during those early years was a little farm house in Mesquite, Texas. My father was a dry farmer. He grew cotton, beans, peanuts and vegetables. My father and oldest brother Cecil plowed the fields with a mule team pulling a hand plow, tilling rows to plant the seeds. Some things like sweet potatoes were planted on small hills, mounds.

We lived in a rural area outside a small town. This was during the Great Depression. Because we were a farm family, we had plenty to eat—not like some folks in the big city. My brothers and sisters were; Cecil, Ecil, Olean, Hazel, Esther and Odell. On our farm, my father grew peanuts as well as vegetables. Come harvest time, they'd pull the whole vine with peanuts still on them. We'd put the vines in the barn. All us kids had to go down to the barn and pick the peanuts off the vines.

We moved to another farm and there we raised corn. Come harvest my mother would send us out around the back of the house to rub the kernels of corn off of the cobs. She had us do enough so she could dry it and, then grind it into corn meal to bake corn bread for a meal.

At that farm we also grew cotton. Father, John Elvie Moore, and Mother, Virgie Savannah Hinshaw Moore, sent us kids out with little cotton sacks at harvest-time. I remember saying to my little brother Odell and my sister Hazel—"Oh, I wish there was a big old truck with a lot of pickers' to pick this cotton, so that I wouldn't have to pick this cotton."

About 3 to five years later, this cotton picking machine came out, with pickers on the front. I remember that it used to leave behind some cotton bolls in the field, but it sure made the cotton harvest a lot easier and faster. Before the machine, my father and all of us had to pick cotton by hand, putting it into long cotton sacks. The seeds in the cotton were sharp and poked our hands. All was done on halves. When the family was hired by other farmers to harvest cotton, each person was paid a dollar a day. Back in those days before Dallas grew into the big city that it is now, there were small tracts of farmland around Mesquite. There were big cotton gins around the area for the growers. My father and mother would take our cotton to the gin and every year they would have all of us a new mattress made for all of us.

In those day's, metal was thick. I remember there was a metal storage building for the Cotton Picking Machine. It was like a big metal barracks or Quonset style of building.

When I was ten years old, we lived in Mesquite, Texas. My mother would have my sister Esther, who was a little older than I, wash the laundry in two big wash tubs. One was for the washing and the other for rinsing. Then the cloths had to be wrung out and hung on the clothes line. I would try to help her, but she would say—" Get away from here! I don't need you to help me!" She sure was high tempered. Esther suffered from bronchial asthma, especialy in the later years of her life.

When I was ten, we attended a little country church called, Hickory Tree Baptist Church. Every Sunday Cecil drove us to church in his Model T. The car was a jalopy! When we got there, Cecil would park right in front of the high porch of the church. That car was a crank-start automobile. When service was over and we got ready to leave, I would get into the car while he crank-started it. He told me, "Put your foot on the brake," because he was in front of the car. But one time I pushed down on the gas pedal! Cecil jumped out of the way and the car and I went up the steps of the porch and crashed into the front of the building. Boy that was a mess! I crashed the car into the front door of the church on a Sunday afternoon! I am glad no one was hurt but everyone was angry.

My faith is Baptist. When I was nine or ten years old, I was saved at a revival meeting by an evangelist named—Prim—Soon afterward, I was baptized at Hickory Tree Baptist Church.

When I was nine or ten years of age, I was to be in the Church's Christmas play. I can play the accordion and I was supposed to play a Christmas carol. I do not recall which one, but when my turn came, I forgot the notes and I played, "When the Roll Is Called up Yonder."

Our family had two old Henry Ford cars; a small truck and a Model T. One time we went on a road trip to Abilene to see my oldest sister Ecil who by that time was married to Albert Harris. She had just had a baby girl, my niece Vivian. She was such a pretty little baby girl.

I must have been either fourteen or fifteen when we lived in Dallas, which had grown a lot. My sister Hazel, her husband and son, Pat Jr. lived out in West Dallas. I would walk to down town Dallas and cross a large bridge on my way to her house. I visited her and her little son. He was such a pretty baby and we were all proud of him.

During those years, Clyde Barrow, Bonnie Parker, L.C. Barrow, and a younger son were running wild in South Dallas and later all over Texas and surrounding states. Bonnie and Clyde started their life of crime by stealing a bit of candy. After that, it seemed every time they turned around the law was chasing after them and accusing them of a crime. They turned out to be a gang of hardened criminals. Bonnie and Clyde were all around me but they never bothered me and I didn't know them. However my brother Cecil knew Clyde's brother, Cecil Barrow. My sister Hazel also knew the Barrow family. The Barrow family attended Hickory Tree Baptist Church and was all good people. The parents were well liked in town and ran a little service station just up the road from where Hazel lived out in West Dallas. Clyde's older brother Cecil Barrow was a quiet fellow not a gangster or a criminal. You never heard of any trouble coming out of the rest of the Barrow family He lived across the street from us when we lived in Dallas. We Later heard that the law had run down Bonnie and Clyde and shot them alongside a highway.

In 1936, we attended the Texas Centennial celebration. I followed Ecil and we sneaked into the fairgrounds by going under the fence. That was her idea, not mine. But we sure did have a wonderful time seeing it all.

When I first started school, it was in Balch Springs, Texas, where a Baptist Church stood. This was where we attended first grade. They served us school lunch on the grounds. I was in one room, and my sister Hazel was in the next room. A boy and I got into a fight! The teacher was more like a baby sitter and she couldn't stop us. Hazel came charging in from the other room and broke it up! I had a Big Red Chief writing tablet that I scribbled in all day.

Next I attended school in Dallas and I even received a creative writing award. I went on a trip with my oldest sister, Ecil down to McAllen, Texas to help a family decorate floats for a parade that summer. My niece Vivian helped but Lorene was only a small girl and too young to work. Before we left for home I had my picture taken in a big Mexican sombrero and a serape. I was 15 and half years old at that time, back in 1936. That was in the years just before world war two and that madman Hitler was in power and the Japanese were stirring up trouble in China. But that was a long way from us and we only heard about it all. That year I wore my first pant suit. It was green.

Odell was a precious little boy when he was a baby and as well when he got older. When he first started school, I was afraid some kid was going to hurt him. I was four years older than Odell. I was worried that some bully was going to hurt him. The school we attended had a playground with big high poles and holders on the end of long ropes coming down from the top pole. We would swing on the playground with one—and I was forever coming down too close to the ground and skinning my knees. In Dallas School, one of the classes that I had was music class. After that year I don't remember being in music class again. I received a writing certificate on January 25th 1935 at Colonial School. My teacher was Milda Leifister and the school principal was B.W. Glasgow. You can say that I had a happy childhood.

You should have seen the bus that we rode to school on. It was an old time kind of bus with a door on the end. It was several miles through the countryside side to get to Colonial School. One place that we passed by on a daily basis was a plant where bricks were made. I don't recall what the other businesses were.

I was a shy girl, but my cousin Bessie used to say this about me; "Oh that Lois, she walks around with her nose up in the air all snooty. When it rains, the rain falls in her nose."

I want to talk some about my Mother, and Father. My mother was raised in the Deep South in Georgia and Alabama. She spoke about seeing wildcats up in the trees when she was young. However later in life she couldn't see very well. She was partially blind. She went up to Oklahoma City to see an eye doctor about her condition but I never knew what condition she had that caused it. I really liked flowers and I still do, mostly feathered. My father had a green-thumb and he could grow flowers and vegetables and just about anything. He was part American Indian, Chickasaw and Scottish. Oh my he had a temper. He might start working on a chair or something. Then if he couldn't get it fixed, he'd get frustrated and angry, lose his temper and tear it up! He said later on, "If I don't control my temper it is going to get me into some real trouble." I told you earlier that we were a farming family. So as well as our crops, my father was a hog farmer. He ate way to much pork ham and bacon which is hog meat and very bad for you. It clogged up his arteries and made him so sick that he died at an early age. He had a small herd of cattle as well. My mother ate pork as well and used to make sausage. She also made lard and soap out of pig oils. We had a smoke house out back. My father would kill and butcher both cattle and hogs so that we would have meat to eat. He would salt the meat and hang it on the walls of the smoke house so as to smoke it and dry it. We had to do this because we didn't have refrigeration and it would have spoiled. If my mother wanted to save some leftovers from lunch till supper that night, she would cover it and put it outside in a little frame window.

One time when I was 15, two boys from down the road a ways, my age, came by the farm. They were driving some sort of old one seat Ford Car; probably a model T. They would drive all over the area. They drove by and asked me if I would like to ride around with them. I said yes." Oh yes." As we drove by the front of our house, wouldn't you know it, my father came out and stopped us. He was really bawling them out. "How dare you pick up my daughter in this car! Lois you get out now and you boys get out of here!" I was just joy riding, that's all. One of the boys remarked that he was going to put lights on that car. Back in those days they didn't have any street lights out in Mesquite where we lived.

Now I want to tell you about my father's mule team. One day those mules broke loose from the plow and starting running away. I guess the reason was that the harness broke after he cracked the whip on them. He would lose his temper at them trying to make them get up and go. I guess those mules got plenty tired of it and broke away, running as fast as they could across the field with my father chasing them.

One Sunday after Church, I went home with another girl and her family. They had a corral with mules penned inside. Mules can be mean and onry as you know. She got into the corral and I saw one of those mules kick her across the face. I didn't go into the corral but her father got her out of there. I felt awful for her.

My father and Cecil were caretakers for Bennett Cemetery, and I often went along with them to help out. I really didn't like to go to that place. But it was a beautiful place, having big trees which were full of singing birds. I still love to hear the birds singing all around. So pretty are their songs.

I remember one time we were on our way home from somewhere. It was my Father and Mother, Odell and I. We came across a car stopped along the side of the road, and there was a drunk guy from somewhere in the neighborhood! When my Father got out of our car, that drunk decided to jump on Dad in a wrestling match! The drunk was laughing the whole time but my father was not! My father got the best of that drunk! He clobbered the drunk and stuffed him back into his car! Then we left. I guess that drunk's family was wondering where he was at that hour of the night. I was really scared that night. It was so dark. There was a half-moon and the sky was clear and the stars were shining brightly in the Texas sky.

During my teen years, two of my cousins would come over with their families to see us. They would bring along their guitars and play old songs of yesteryear. My Father and Mother and all of us loved to hear them sing; especially my Father. We had some kind of a wind organ as well. It had foot pedals that you would push when you played it. We had a Ventrola phonograph and Cecil had a bunch of seventy-eight speed records. He loaned them to one of our cousins who failed to return them. So one day my brother decided to ask her to give them back. She replied, "One of the boys took them down to the junk yard." Cecil was very upset over that! I do not know what happened to the phonograph or the wind organ. I remember on one of those records was, "Johnson's Old Gray Mule," *"Ticklish Rubin,"* and,

"Uncle Josh's Laughing Song." These songs were written by a fellow called, "Uncle Josh."

Another time on the farm in Mesquite, Cecil and I and our Father were walking across a large field to a big pasture. The owner of that land was grazing a big mean Brahma Bull. Before we got to our fence we heard Ole Bill (the bull) snorting at us! I was real scared! Mother shouted, "Hurry and get through the fence! Old Bill is coming!" I put my right foot through the barbed wire and cut my leg. The cut was 2 ½ inches long and it hurt! I have a scar on my ankle from it to this day. All of us made it across the fence as Old Bill was charging across the meadow! We sure took a big chance. It was almost a dare to cross Old Bill's pasture. Maybe the owner of that bull didn't keep him there all the time and I really don't think my Father knew Old Bill was there. Those times were hard and I guess a lot of people had to take dares just to survive in the Great Depression and the dust bowel.

One time I baked the bread for our family. We had a big wood cook stove. For heat in the winter we had a wood burning heater. Bringing firewood was part of the chores we had on the farm. When it was cold, every morning, Cecil would rise early and kindle the fire for us all. Storms coming down from the north we called, *"Ole blue northers."*

One of our neighbors was a man named, "Saul Davison." Mrs. Davison used to call my little brother Odell, *"Ah-dell."*

I remember Cecil, when he was 16 years of age, putting together an Ear phone radio. It could only be heard through a set of earphones. I do not know where he got the kit or how he accomplished this. But we saw him listening to it through his ear phones and we could hear the broadcast.

From my earliest childhood memories, I remembered my father smoking his pipe. I can still recall the sweet aroma of the Dermot Tobacco that he smoked. It used to come in little sacks and he would buy it down at the general store there in Mesquite. One day I got into his tobacco to smell of it. Little Odell was right there close by. Later Father found that it had been opened. "Which one of you opened this new bag of Tobacco?" It was me but I was afraid to admit it and Odell, knowing it was me replied, "We don't know who it was?" That was the last we heard about it from Father.

The place where we lived was close to some railroad tracks, and we could see the train stop shelter where people would come and sit to wait. In those days there were still a lot of passenger trains around. As the years went by in my life, I saw all of those things change and everyone switching over to buses. Now all that is left is Amtrak. There all along the tracks many beautiful wild flowers were growing on both sides of the rails. That place was lush and green but very hot and humid in the summer. One of my little nieces loved to pick the wild flowers for my oldest sister Ecil. It was her daughter Vivian. Ecil would get upset with her over something and. I'd say to Vivian, "Oh come, don't you want to pick wildflowers alongside of the railroad tracks? "Oh I'd like that," she replied and away we would go, picking wildflowers. Now these days you don't dare go up on the tracks because the trains are moving too fast.

Not too far from our house across the tracks, a man and his wife ran a little country store. It was the same place where my father purchased his pipe tobacco

Further up the road there was another Mercantile Store run by Mrs. Zipp. The first thing I knew everyone was calling her, "Lady Zipp. She Zips in and zips out." For some strange reason she had a commode outside by the store.

In another direction across the way there was a Christian Church. I would take my niece Vivian to church there on Sundays when we couldn't get to Hickory Tree Baptist church, which was several miles away. Other times I would ride with Cecil to another Church called, "Forest Avenue Baptist Church." By that time we had moved into town and it was just up the street from us.

Someone in our family gave me a pretty dress. I like it and wore it to church. It was a little tight around the waist, but regardless of that I still wore it to church because I liked it. By that time Mother had gotten to where she couldn't sew for us. She had to give up on sewing because of her worsening eyesight. But she loved us and tried for as long as she could. As for myself, I didn't have the gift or talent to sew. However my daughter Linda sure does. I remember one little place close by where we were taught by plating rows of materials of different colors; by means of a little wood plating machine. We were sewing the plated materials together to make a rug by hand.

As I look back on it all, it seems that a lot of water has passed under this bridge which is my life. Lots of events have happened and I want them to be remembered, not for myself, but for the sake of future generations of our family

The following story is a true account of how the Lord came to our Mother and placed his anointing on her life

GOD'S GENTLE TOUCH

When I was but a little girl, My Lord and Master said to me, "Now girl, you were born to serve the Lord. Now you listen for a still small voice that one day may come to you and say, Listen to me. I am God speaking to you. You'll do as I say. I'll touch you one day. I'll anoint you with my power on high to go out in all the hills and valleys and all the byways of life. My strength I'll give to you. New courage, you have an ample supply. I'll make you a blessing, to give to others my redeeming love. My sheep were stolen away from me oh, oh so long ago. But you can help me to bring them back to my sheepfold."

When I grew to womanhood and had a family, He came and touched me with his anointing hand. I felt God's power going through my shoulder and down into my arm and hand. When God came down and gently touched my shoulder, I felt His presence standing over me.

Later He came to me a couple of times. He came and He walked all around as I was resting on a peaceful afternoon. I didn't see His face but I heard Him walking. When I awoke, I knew that it had been God. God had been at our place and had come to visit us. Oh how beautiful it is to hear God walking in the cool of the evening. Oh how precious are the feet of Jesus, our Lord and Master, our God.

I had been so afraid of life; living in fear and He came to give me His peace. Since then my life has been different. My life hasn't been my own since then.

I have been redeemed, bought with a price, to do the work God has set for me to do while living on this earth; with His guiding hand upon be, bringing God's sheep back to the fold.

"My peace I give to you." These are the words God spoke to me. "My peace I give to you."

January 1973.

Writing Certificate

This is to Certify that _Lois Moore_
has faithfully applied the principles of muscular movement to all written
work while in the elementary grades of the Dallas Public Schools, and
is therefore entitled to this Certificate in official recognition thereof.

Given at Dallas, Texas, this __ day of _January_ 193_

Principal

Teacher

School

Superintendent

Supervisor of Writing

"Writing maketh an exact man."—Bacon.

15

4A | Saturday
October 23, 2004
CURRENT-ARGUS

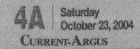

CURRENT-ARGUS

A politically independent newspaper in its 115th year.

Rockford M. Hayes
Publisher

David Giuliani
Managing Editor

Serving Eddy County

A Gannett Newspaper

Sharing poetry about rose

Editor:

I pray you will like and enjoy this poetry essay. May you be blessed.

The Rose

I once saw a rose upon a rose bush, standing tall and proud. Its beauty was as crimson. Its petals they hung as bright mistletoe upon this bush of the roses.

The roses that were clustered all around this rose bush were nothing compared to this one bright rose of beauty shining forth as in crimson love for all other roses. This tall rose of pure beauty talked to God, the Father above, about all these clustered problems these little roses have in their state of blossomed blight.

This rose I saw upon the bush was standing tall in God, and by his eternal light. Their protector and spokesman to God, for they, the roses.

This mighty rose of great beauty and lights, its flower and fragrance of pure love will stand forever in bloom in God's heavenly kingdom of love and light.

Its petals spoke out to God in love for all these, the roses, in their state of sin's plight. This rose of beauty, its love and care for all others were like a great light to shine upon these helpless roses.

Yes, today this tall rose of beauty is in prayer to God, for all the little roses who will one day reign with him forever.

Who is the tall red rose of majesty with beauty? It's Jesus, our Heavenly Rose of Sharon.

Yes, today he is our protector and we are all in his care. One day, we shall, all the roses, shine forth in his presence, into his eternal heavenly glory, in his presence of joy and light, into a lasting kingdom.

LOIS NEWCOMB
Carlsbad

A PHONE CALL HOME

A prayer is like a phone call home. Do you remember a time when you were away from home? You found you were missing your loved ones. You then decided to call home. The phone is ringing—you are sad. The lonely feeling for home is very real. As you stand waiting for someone to answer at the other end, you know you have dialed the right number. Then suddenly, the silence is broken. You hear a comforting voice saying, "Hello there."

When we pray, it is like a phone call to heaven. We know we have the right number, for our hearts are in Jesus. Oh what joy to know that God is on the other end of our line. We know that when we call home to Heaven God is always there, waiting for us to call, saying to us," Hello there." We should always remember to call our loved ones back home by phone. But we as Christians should always remember to call daily on our prayer phone to God. It is our duty to communicate in order to have a happier life without sadness.

Most of us may remember how we missed our loved ones when we were away. It is the same way with God. He misses us talking with him when Christians neglect to pray. When we fail to call, He stands waiting for us to call. He knows all of our wants and needs, but He wants to hear our petition. When we call home to Heaven, we can hear his warm voice saying," Hello there." God will always answer, but we must remember to call. God however answers our petitions in His own time. If He doesn't grant you petition immediately, don't give up so soon. For if you continue to ring God's line, He will not only answer, but will grant our wish (if it is in accordance with His will). But it is always good to call God and hear Him say, "Hello there."

THE ROLLING HILLS

The rolling hills we love so well with wildflowers all posed; green grass and gentle roe in natural beauty for these rolling hills.

Life spands and night comes. Then open fields their soft candlelight glows.

Day comes with sunlight. Jonquil, amber, pink and red roses scattered over these rolling hills.

Daydream of distant flight, children play in the prairie light. Time goes on wings that fly while summits grow in distant time.

The Orchards quale a mellow tone; spirit thrives in trees of green. Bells toll at meadows gulch over sound of water, and on to Ransom's Pass.

Days pass, a restful time. Night comes, a springlette wails. Earth's sods in cascades reach, while daffodils grow in sunlight's gleam.

Mockingbird sings its song of love while cattle graze in lowlands lull; a pleasing sight; a gentle breeze, pleasure of a growing doe, grazing from its hamlets knoll, gazing far in hopeful dream.

"Dawns awake"—coming from the bell tower and dome. In these hills are chimes, ringing out in praise of our Lord God, while the dells lift up evergreen petals pointing upward to the sky.

Phantoms race through clouds above these ancient hills, clouds in picturesque form.

Standing high on a hilltop is a beautiful mansion, so lovely and so pretty; a mansion on a hilltop in these lovely hills of God's Creation.

A river of cold fresh water is ever flowing downward out of these hills into valleys below, keeping things that grow so green and ever so lovely.

God's hills and His alone, all made for mankind to love and to roam.

In freedom's dress are these ancient hills of trust (*meeting place*). Yes, pleasing in God's sight is man's zest for in these colorful hills. He gave them to us to use and to have and behold and so to enjoy; to enjoy God's great handiwork of love for all mankind. Yes, our God of love; for that is what we love.

December 28th, 1972☺

THE ROSE,
A PICTURE STORY OF THE MESSIAH

I once saw a rose upon a rose bush, standing tall and proud. Its beauty was as crimson. Its petals; they hung as bright mistletoe upon this bush of the roses.

The roses that were clustered all around the bush were nothing compared to this one bring rose of beauty, shining forth as in crimson love for all the other roses. This tall rose of pure beauty talked to God the Father about all these clustered problems these little roses have in their sate of blossomed blight.

This rose I saw upon the bush was standing tall in God, and by His Eternal Light. This great rose is their protector and spokesman to God for the smaller roses.

This mighty rose of great beauty and light, its flower and fragrance of pure love will stand forever in bloom in God's Heavenly Kingdom of Love and Light.

Its petals spoke out to God in love for all these, the roses, in their state of sins plight. This rose of beauty, its love and care for the others were like a great light shining upon these helpless roses.

Yes, today this tall rose of beauty is in prayer to God, for all the little roses who will one day reign with him forever.

Who is this tall Rose of Majesty with beauty? It is Jesus, our Heavenly Rose of Sha'ron.

Yes, today He is our protector and we are all in His care. One day we shall, all of us, the roses, shine forth in His presence, into His eternal heavenly glory; in His presence of joy and light into an everlasting Kingdom.

February 1973.✿

JUST BECAUSE

I once was in a sea of darkness, and I knew not where or how to go; But the Lord came down and He sought me. He lifted me up, made well my troubled life.

He saved my soul, revealed His mercy thru His dear Son on Calvary. He died so that I could live forever on God's Eternal Golden Shore.

Jesus paid the price for my redemption by dying on the cross for me; He shed His blood and gave me salvation and loosed me from earth's power of sin.

I trusted in His death payment to save me by grace thru faith. He forgave me and not of works could I have boasted; Twas a gift from God's own son.

I was not worthy of redemption but Jesus came and gave me new life; His love for me was far greater than tongues on earth can ever tell. And now I have eternal salvation for Jesus came and died for me. *And just because* He first loved me, I owe my life, my all to him.

For God so loved the world that He gave His only begotten son. That whosoever would believe in Jesus shall never perish, but have everlasting life. God said that whoever would believe in Jesus shall never perish but have life everlasting. He'll pardon you now and forever. Just trust and believe in Him today.

1977

Editor's Note: *This next poem is a lesson on the dangers of men falling into the trap of prostitution, lust and alcoholism. The character Sam represents men in general, and Mira Dix can represent all the temptations each and every one of us faces. Whether it be drugs and alcohol or prostitution, adultery and pornography. My mother new the value of chastity and purity and warned of the regret one would feel, when wasting the gift of physical intimacy with whores and whore mongers. Our Ruby, as Mother call that one special person that is our soul mate, is the one for whom we should wait for, lest we suffer awful hardships and regret because we did not follow God's Holy Law of Matrimony. In her honorable way, our Mother taught this lesson without having to use the vulgarity of modern society.*

IN THE MUD WITH MIRA DIX

Sam! Don't fall in the mud with Mira Dix! Don't listen when she calls saying, "Come sit under my apple tree with me."

Now sure as you do Sam, you'll be sorry. You will find yourself going down! And oh the fall! How hard it will surely be to find your way up again after you go down Sam!

Sam, just one step at a time downwards is all it takes. One day you will wake up and find yourself stuck fast in the mud Sam. Sam with Mira Dix stuck in miry clay! Yes, for sure it will be hard to find your way up again. But you can make it; but oh so hard! But you can make it.

Right now Sam, you must be strong now and on your guard Sam; and be on the alert. Watch out for Mira Dix.

Now first off Sam, just be sure you're in the right and you'll not heed to her call.

Sam there is many pebbles on a beach. Always stop and look and listen before you leap, for there is one true ruby one day for you if you will not listen to Mira Dix.

But today Sam, watch out; God's whistle will blow one day, so heed now to His calling before it's too late Sam!

So Sam when you hear, "Come sit under my apple tree with me;" no Sam! Don't you do it for there's mud under her apple tree. For mud is mud. Now you listen Sam! As sure as you do, you will find yourself going down, down, down! Then one day your Ruby will come along and then you'll be sorry for heeding the call of Mira Dix.

Yes Sam, also with that first drink; that is when you'll find yourself heading down. So Sam! Wake up! Wake up! Awake out of your trance before you find yourself down in the mud with Mira Dix and stuck for sure in miry clay.

But if you do Sam, remember you can never crawl back up on your own nor pull yourself back up by your own bootstraps. Only through God's only Son Jesus. Let him strengthen and help you. Let Him help you climb up and let him be your guide.

July 24ᵗʰ 1979.

JESUS THE LIGHT

(IT IS HE)

IT IS HE who can calm the waves at sea and does set His Light upon lonely seashores.

IT IS HE; Jesus our true light

IT IS HE; He is the Lighthouse that shines out over the deepest seas at night, to guide the ships to shore from the open sea.

IT IS HE; The Light and the rescue of the perishing souls out on life's seas and upon its sandy beaches of time.

IT IS HE who can calm our angry waves and say," *Peace, be still,*" when things come our way that often upset us.

IT IS HE who can say," *My peace I can give to you.*"—If we be still a moment and take time to listen for his voice; through His marvelous grace and love for us, we can ride the angry waves at sea.

IT IS HE who is the lighthouse guiding us over the rough waves and to life's shore, we can be overcomers. With him as the Lighthouse we also can help rescue those who perish be it on land, at sea or up in the air.

IT IS HE who with his help we can ourselves become lighthouses for Jesus, bringing in lost souls to safety from life's seas and onto its sandy seashore; to the harbor of life and safety in Jesus and His Holy Word. For His words are God given and God's breathe of life, through his own Son, Jesus—His word is Jesus.

IT IS HE Jesus, God given, God's breath to rescue lost souls out on the deepest of seas and upon all life's sandy beaches of time. It is a picture of the stresses of life and our daily climb upward in Jesus and in overcoming obstacles.

IT IS HE who is the only way—Jesus, He is the way; for he is our light and our lighthouse in our time. He can be our personal light and guide.

IT IS HE who can rescue the perishing and save souls from any situation, if we but trust in Him on sea or in the air.

IT IS HE who in the Bible tells us to," *Go ye into all the world and tell the Gospel"* story of Jesus the Christ; telling of His love for them through His Heavenly Light and in He who is the Lighthouse. To tell what He has done for me, that He has rescued even me (an unworthy sinner); that Jesus is now my personal light and that He is the Light of the whole world.

IT IS HE who can rescue even you and me and calm our waves at sea.

IT IS HE who can daily calm your way and waves of distress in life, simply by accepting the Light of Jesus and taking Him as your Lighthouse upon your sea of life.

IT IS HE who through His love, mercy and through His grace, we can in some way go into the entire world and tell the Gospel story of Jesus Christ; we who have been redeemed.

January 4th, 1985✡

HE IS LIGHT

In every dark cloud in the sky, there is a silver lining; for we see the rainbow as it shines in the clouds. Through the rainclouds there is light

God is the light at the end of all dark skies. He is our rainbow of hope; our silver lining in a cloud of night. He is our morning light. For joy cometh in His Light of Day.

Jesus is the light of our soul. He is a lamp unto our feet and a light unto our pathway. He is a good shepherd for He leadeth.

In trials of life, He cares and He knows each heart and even sees a tear that may fall, as He sees and knows each raindrop that falls from a cloud in the sky.

He is our refuge in a time of storm out on life's seas for He is an alcove, our shelter upon life's rocky shore.

He is our laughter and our smile for He dwells within a soul. He is our joy and our happiness for He is Love and He is Life. God is light and He is hope. He is our only hope for life eternal.

John 3:16 For God so loved the world, that he gave his only begotten Son, that whosoever believeth in him should not perish, but have everlasting life. *(King James Version)*

He is life everlasting and life eternal, for whosoever that believeth in Him.

A Prose in Thought

February 28,1988

BEAUTIFUL ROSES

Thoughts for Today

Today when I look around and see the beautiful roses growing on a lawn or in a rose garden, I see their beauty. They remind me of a true Christian. They picture our way and walk through life while living on earth.

A rose grows with its beauty in both color and design. Roses exemplify truth and beauty as we live today. But along with beauty and design, a rose has thorns. We as Christians will have the thorns of life along the way. The thorns represent trials and tribulations in our lives.

Christians should live today and strive to grow in God's Spirit. Through His grace and love, we can do this. He wants us to grow to reach a maturity in Him. In doing this, we must remember that there may be earthly trials of thorns in our lives. We may be tried and tempted in reaching God's heavenly goals for us.

Many times God may allow things to come our way only to make us grown in Him. We need this to keep us from standing still.

Now in Heaven, rewards will be given. Remembering this, we should not stand still in our actions for God. We should keep on striving for our heavenly goals regardless of the thorns. And always remember, a rose will always have thorns as it grows.

Jesus, our great Rose of Sha'ron, suffered many thorns (trials) for us. He suffered and died on the cross. He never stopped and stood still. He endured these thorns for us. The crown of thorns they placed upon His head. He suffered just for us. He did this willingly so we could have eternal life in heaven; a life with a new body that will be likened unto Him.

We will endure these things on earth, but in heaven there will be no more thorns. We, as God's roses, will have no thorns and Jesus will be our eternal, "Rose of Sha'ron."

In heaven there will be no trials of life; only comfort, peace, joy, and happiness with a beautiful crown of life. Today, we have joy and happiness for short lived times. Then again come the thorns of life which pierce us as we live; the good with the bad. But here we can't have the good without the bad to make us grow; to keep on growing, so as not to stand still. In heaven all will be different for us. All is good. There will be no negatives, only positives and no thorns of sin will enter into heavens gates.

We as believers can be compared to God's little roses. In heaven we can see many beautiful roses actually growing in a holy garden; real roses that are growing in real gardens along with many other flowers; flowers that bloom in their beauty only in heaven.

A rose also represents each born-again believer in Jesus of all nationalities and colors; those who one day will inherit heaven as their home. We are all God's little roses and Jesus is our heavenly "Rose of Sha'ron.

Aug 25th, 1990.

LET THE SUN COME SHINING THROUGH

Thoughts for Today

Many people today often talk of troubles and trials all over the land. Very often we forget the good things of life. Let us turn around and see God's beauty in our lives that He has given us. His light, His love and care through all these things.

Now if we but try to look for God's help and guidance we will see many good things of life that are in our lives for us today.

Let us stop and think and give God credit and our thanks for all blessings of life.

Let us praise the Lord in everything, for in so doing all these things of strife will fall into our backgrounds and take a back seat in all our lives. Our thoughts will then be brighter all day. The beautiful sun will then come shining through.

August 6th, 1991.

HOPE

I.

Today having hope in our lives is very important for us. When there is hope, we have light. Then we go forward as looking for better things to come.When trials of life come our way, with hope we will come through to their end with flying colors; for we see light at the end of tunnels. For our eternal hope has been set in Jesus.

But know this—a deep peace of mind with hope and joy for our souls cannot come unless we on our part have made a true repentance toward God and Jesus Christ. Yes, to know Jesus is to know God, and knowing this, we have true peace of mind; then and only then, peace with hope comes to us.

II.

Yes, a true inner peace, God Eternal within us can bring us hope with true joy and happiness along with love. Today God speaks through His word, our Bible, and many times to us in a *"Still Small Voice."* He speaks to our soul's inner mind. Today if you hear His voice, then stop, listen, and hear His word.

Take action today and make a decision for God and He will shine with His light and love and give true hope today, which will bring eternal hope.

Now let us remember that our deep faith and hope is only found in God; and through His love for us. He is our only way to true life and hope with happiness.

September 11, 1992.

LINDA THE BEAUTIFUL

Linda is my daughter. She's very nice and kind. She makes the prettiest things for home and for family and friends.

Her talent is outstanding, given to her by God. Now God has made her a beautiful person with a heart of gold. She cares for others in her very own and special way.

The best of all I see in Linda is that she is my own sweet daughter who always tries to stand by Mom and all her family in her nice and caring way.

Now her devotion to God is tops for daily she tries to please her Lord in the little things that she does for others; in her own special way, always with a smile. That is great.

Yes, Linda is a beautiful daughter! A daughter to be proud of! We, her family all love her. Yes, more and more each day. As the years go by, may God always bless our Linda; bless her in His best ways and in His will for her.

Yes, Linda is her name; a name that means, *"Beautiful"*. A name that is just right for Linda, chosen for her by me, her Mom, who thinks that she is great in a very special way.

February 24, 1993

GLENDA

Glenda is my own beautiful daughter—Glenda Joyce is her name. "Glen" or "Glenda" means, *"water or a body of water, a glen.* "Joyce" means to *"rejoice"* or *"joy,"* for joy cometh in the morning.

Yes, Glenda was given to me by God for a special purpose for Him in His will and service. God has given her a very special talent; a gift to be used for His honor and for His glory and praise. A gift to be able to teach little children about Jesus, to rescue their souls from waters of life or from the sands of time, so that one day they may awake to a morning of eternal joy.

Yes I feel God has chosen her for a very special purpose—to work with little children; to help little children to find a real purpose in their lives for God, so that they may have a real joy and happiness in their own little lives. And teach them daily to live for Jesus. Yes in Christian school, to teach them God's way of life and for her own now in a home school Christian program in curriculum studies and in Bible.

Glenda is a very faithful person in her teaching of little children and her own to uphold and honor God's work and Jesus Christ. She is a faithful mother who daily stands by her own young children, to lead and to guide them daily in truth and in righteousness And she always helps Mom—Mother too—in little things I may need in life when she is able to do so.

Yes I feel that Glenda is using her gifts and talents for God's purpose for her and in opportunities in life; she uses His service. I feel that Glenda is doing

God's will, being what God wants her to be in Him, and using her talents well. Talents are to be used and not buried in the sands of time.

We, her family all love her and we are proud of Glenda. We appreciate her using her spiritual gifts from God to honor Him and uplift the name of Jesus; honoring Jesus in all walks of her life; to uplift His name above in things of heaven and on earth.

Glenda loves to have a nice time; a nice time yes but in our Lord Jesus Christ, in fellowship with others; with other believers in God's service. By using her talent that God has given her; she has helped little children to know Jesus; believing in and knowing Jesus Christ in their own lives. This is so that their own little souls and lives may be conformed to the likeness of Jesus in meaning and character. God loves all the little children of the world.

March 8, 1993

VICKIE

Vickie is her name and she is a very special lady for God with a true heart of gold and beautiful person for Jesus and in Jesus

Vickie is a name just right for her which means "Victory in Jesus;" a name chosen for her by her Mom. Now God has given Vickie a talent, a very special gift from Him; beautiful gift in gospel song and music.

Now Vickie is using her talent for the glory of God; to glorify Jesus; a God-given talent to achieve His will and His purpose for her in her life today.

Now Vickie is striving to live for Jesus each day the best she knows how. Vicky is an over-comer in Jesus, God's only Son, and going forward each day for Jesus. Vicki has not buried her talent in the sands of time like many do today, but is using it for Jesus in order to glorify Him.

Yes, God has redeemed Vickie through His son Jesus. God loves Vickie and Vickie loves God; for he died for Vickie and gave His life for her, and arose for Vickie.

Now Vickie by faith accepted Jesus, God's only son, into her heart and life at the age of 16. She now has a real purpose in life; a desire to go forward; to live for Jesus and do His will.

Vickie loves music and loves to sing; singing daily His praises in her life. She loves to sing gospel songs with messages that tell others messages from God in songs for them. How that God also loves them very much.

Now Vickie has a wonderful husband, Gary Davis, Vickie's God-given life-partner for her. Vickie loves Gary dearly and Gary loves Vickie, for God gave them each other to go forward together, accomplishing His will as they both live their lives together for Him.

Now Gary is a very nice and kind person just like Vickie for Jesus, and in his daily walk with God, like her, he is not hiding his talents or burying them in the sands of time. He is going forward daily for Jesus. Yes, together they go forward in Jesus.

May God always bless Gary and Vickie Davis with His grace, love and beauty, through His only Eternal Son Jesus. May God's sunlight of love shine down from heaven upon them, always helping them throughout this life and with their going forward in His will for them.

Written on behalf of Gary and Vickie Davis,
of Carlsbad, New Mexico, June 30th 1993.

THIS LITTLE RED, RED ROSE

This little red rose is sent to you, a token of the Rose of Sha'ron. It is sent to you in Christian love and faith in Jesus. May it brighten up your day bringing you a sweet peace and joy within; within your heart, mind and soul, today.

This little red, red rose is sent to bring a smile upon your face for you are remembered in our prayer that good blessings from above will be for you. May you go forth to honor and praise His Holy Name, Jesus, our red, red rose of Sha'ron. It is He who can fill you with joy and happiness daily as you go forth to honor and serve Him; each day in work or play.

May our Rose of Sha'ron be remembered daily in your life and in all our lives; of His death and resurrection and that He died for all. May you be blessed in His will and way for you through His eternal love for you.

May we all go forth daily to be a blessing for others in some little way or another and to be a blessing to the whole world; a testimony to our Heavenly King of Glory, our red, red rose whose name is Jesus. Yes, let us go forth in faith and honor to Him who cares for our eternal souls

As you receive this little red, red rose, please try to remember we here care for you. I can say we love you from Jesus, our red, red rose of Sha'ron. May we remember He is our light, lighting up our pathways in the night. I can say today, may we all go forth in service for Him who truly loves us, by and through His Heavenly amazing grace. Through His love and grace, may we go forth.

May we go forth with a love and zeal, with a smile upon our faces in service for our red, red Rose of Sha'ron, King of Glory. May we all go forth in honor to His name with believing because He lives, we shall live.

Yes, may this little rose sent to you today bring a happy smile upon your face and may we all go forth with a smile to show the world we care.

May 10th, 1996

THE RAIN

Oh, the beauty of the rain that falls upon the earthen deserts of sand. The rain that makes pretty wild flowers and cactus grow.

A delight to see and a joy to all who may walk the desert pathways of life

The rain is a treasure from our God of Love. He makes all things grow for mankind. Without the rain no lovely things grow. No rainbows would be in the sky to decorate nature in its beauty for all to see.

The rain is a gift of God's love to all

October 15th, 2002

This last poem written by our mother is a very fitting epilogue to this book and I don't think that it is any coincidence that it was written in the order that it was. Especially the last paragraph which is a candid personal conviction, that she thought she had failed to meet her own high standard of Christian Religious practice. I suggest that everyone who reads her book, endeavor to at least in some measure, put into practice the kind of love and care that she has shown for others in her life. You can feel her love, warmth, humbleness and kindness in very word of prose that is in her book. By doing so, all of can live the lives that Lois Newcomb espouses and thus bring her honor.

BELIEVERS

During my life I have not measured up to my own standard of God's love. God is a Holy God. As servants of God through His son Jesus, we will not be holy until we see Jesus face to face. Today He sees us as righteous servants, through Jesus through His shed blood when He died for all on a cruel cross to cover our sins. From a fallen state, receiving Christ we come back to His love, which gives us a confidence in Jesus.

We can pray in Jesus' name for God to help us. We can pray to Jesus, God's son, to help us have confidence in ourselves. He hears our pleas and gives us His confidence to go forward and serve Him. Jesus is our eternal shield of faith and He sees our sins covered by His blood and answers our prayers. He makes us worthy to go forward in Him to serve. When we know Him, He will be our peace, joy and happiness. He gives us abilities and is understanding. He gives us a gentle spirit, for he is long-suffering toward us.

He gives us a meekness and kindness of heart as well as a humble spirit, for He is love. He is charity. He tells us to love our neighbor as ourselves. How much do we say, we love? How much do we love ourselves? Let God love be your answer. Confide in God that He may show you the way to a higher love, then grow in Jesus.

When we ask, He will give us confidence in a surrendered will toward Jesus, to serve Him.

I know today that I have failed many times and have come up short of His glory. I have lacked confidence in myself and my being and have failed many times to go forward as I should. God is our armor of love and light and He is our eternal Father and guide. He will show us the way to a higher love if we just let Him. This applies to me as well. I must let God show me the way. He will see my need and help me. He will see your need and help you. He will give us the strength to go forward in this life.

August 2002

THE END.

Printed in the United States
By Bookmasters